You've Screwed Up.
Now What?!

You've Screwed Up. Now What?!

How to maintain your job and dignity after a major screw up.

Larry D. Kelley

iUniverse, Inc.
New York Lincoln Shanghai

You've Screwed Up. Now What?!
How to maintain your job and dignity after a major screw up.

Copyright © 2007 by Larry D. Kelley

All rights reserved. No part of this book may be used or reproduced by any means, graphic, electronic, or mechanical, including photocopying, recording, taping or by any information storage retrieval system without the written permission of the publisher except in the case of brief quotations embodied in critical articles and reviews.

iUniverse books may be ordered through booksellers or by contacting:

iUniverse
2021 Pine Lake Road, Suite 100
Lincoln, NE 68512
www.iuniverse.com
1-800-Authors (1-800-288-4677)

Because of the dynamic nature of the Internet, any Web addresses or links contained in this book may have changed since publication and may no longer be valid.

The views expressed in this work are solely those of the author and do not necessarily reflect the views of the publisher, and the publisher hereby disclaims any responsibility for them.

ISBN: 978-0-595-45370-2 (pbk)
ISBN: 978-0-595-69457-0 (cloth)
ISBN: 978-0-595-89681-3 (ebk)

Printed in the United States of America

Contents

Chapter 1: Why This Book?..1
Chapter 2: Seven Deadly Business Screw-ups 5
Chapter 3: What to do, now that you've screwed-up......................13
Chapter 4: The Budget Screw-up 21
Chapter 5: The Deadline Screw-up 27
Chapter 6: The Presentation Screw-up 37
Chapter 7: Screwed-up Plan 45
Chapter 8: Company Party 55
Chapter 9: The Hiring Screw-up..67
Chapter 10: You've Signed Something You Shouldn't Have 79

Chapter 1

Why This Book?

This is a book about screwing up at work. If you are reading this book to learn about success or how to prevent a catastrophe, you should stop now and go get a latte. This book is not about *prevention*. It is about *preservation*.

There are a million books on success. But let's face it, for every successful person, there are millions that have screwed-up, like you and me. This is a book for the rest of us because, while we may dream about success, we are darned well going to screw something up. In fact, you may be committing a big screw-up right now. It can happen that quickly. With so many possible screw-ups, I have had to confine the topic to a specific category. Otherwise, who knows how long this could be and, frankly, endless writing might be considered a screw-up in and of itself.

Prevention versus Preservation

As I previously mentioned, there is a lot written on how to succeed. There are also some books dealing with how to prevent failure. That is their take on how to be successful. Like football, most people like to see the offense score. So, there go those "success books" with a million ways that great individuals have scored. However, sometimes preventing a gaffe is also a road to success. If you don't fail, you don't necessary succeed but, then again, if you can prevent major foul-ups, you are more than likely to have that success checkmark.

This book is written from a preservation viewpoint. I am assuming that you have screwed-up. Trust me, that is a pretty good assumption. I didn't have to go too far to figure that one out. My goal is to make sure that when you do screw-up (and you will), that it doesn't become your last screw-up. We are all about preservation here. I want you to keep your miserable job that you will have not a great chance of really succeeding at. That is why this book is about how to maintain your job and your dignity.

Keeping the job or having the option to quit on your own terms is a lot better than being marked with a scarlet red letter "S" for the rest of your life. We are not talking about Superman here. We are talking about Super blunder. We will cover the options you have once you make your screw-up. There are some basic ways to keep that job and some shred of dignity. Warning: One size does not fit all. We will discuss these "keep on keeping on" methods with various screw-ups.

Screw-ups vs. Failure

That brings me to my favorite topic, the screw-up. Now, it is important to understand the difference between a screw-up and a failure. Again, if you are reading this book to understand how to overcome your failures, shut this book now and go buy one of the millions of books on this topic. No, this book is not going to help you overcome your failures. If all you had to do was overcome a measly failure or two, that would be a cakewalk.

No folks, we are talking screw-ups here. Let me give you some quick definitions. I fail just about every Saturday to break 100 on the golf course.

However, on one day, when I actually did break 100 on the golf course, I also broke my golf cart by driving it into a creek. Now that is a screw-up.

All the great ones had failures. Benjamin Franklin just about got killed with the key and the kite. George Washington had his butt kicked by the British. Babe Ruth didn't get a hit two out of three times he was at the plate. Yes, overcoming failure is a test of character. All the great ones did it. Yak. Yak. Yak.

What if George Washington hit his snooze alarm and overslept when he was going to ford the Delaware River. Can you say; "Hail to the Queen." Because, that would have been one monumental screw-up. What if Benjamin Franklin had dropped his pipe on the Declaration of Independence? What do you think we would be declaring then? Or if the Babe was caught trying on women's underwear in the locker room. Perhaps, that was how he got that Babe nickname, huh?

Anyway, these are examples of screw-ups. Screw-ups are not failures. Failures are just not quite getting there. In a failure, you are trying your best but some outside force is against you. In a screw-up, you aren't trying and the only force against you is you. Yes, Pogo, we have seen the enemy and they are us.

The Business of Screw-ups

Screw-ups are our business and this is the business of screw-ups. Easy to understand, isn't it. There are so many screw-ups in the world that we had to draw a line in the sand. So, this book is about common, or uncommon, as the case may be, screw-ups that happen at work.

If this book is wildly successful (ok, if it sells some copies to keep the publisher happy), then we will devote my resources to discussing screw-ups at school or relationships or walking the dog. Yes, you can screw-up walking the dog. Ever have one of those dog doo baggies break on you. Well, those baggies are a screw-up waiting to happen.

Actually, my next sequel may be great movie screw-ups. For example, when Igor brought Doctor Frankstein the brain of "Abby Normal" in the movie, *Young Frankenstein*, that was a classic screw-up. Or Flounder, in the movie, *Animal House*, taking the guys for a ride in his brother's brand-new car that ends up getting smashed beyond comprehension on their infamous road trip. In fact, as Flounder is weeping, looking at the smashed car, Otter tells Flounder, "Flounder, you screwed-up, you trusted us." That is a classic line. It is that type of event that has inspired this book.

So, now you know the wherefores and whys of this book, let's get in to how to deal with those business screw-ups that you know all too well.

Screw Up Book

Chapter 2

Seven Deadly Business Screw-ups

After extensive research, I have come up with the seven most common and potentially lethal business screw-ups. OK, I know, the seven deadly sins parallel is a bit lame but, hey, this is a book about screw-ups after all. If you want some uplifting success fluff piece, go hit any bookstore. There are millions of them.

Like any list; there can be debate and rancor over what should be on it and what might be left off. Suffice it to say; the following seven deadly business sins are happening with such regularity that you may think that they aren't even screw-ups. Some of these happen so often in some companies that they have actually become a part of the fabric of the company.

On Time and On Budget

My first two deadly business screw-ups that we will dive into are the deadly duo. Although I devote a chapter to each, they do seem to go together. This is because most companies have a very difficult time being on time and on budget with just about any project that they do.

In fact, most companies say you typically can't have one with the other.

"You want that when? Tomorrow!!! Well, that is going to cost you extra."

Vendors usually are inept. Use that knowledge to your advantage.

Unfortunately, in our age of FedEx, Dell and the Internet, the margin for being on time has shrunk to the nanosecond. It is not enough to be on time these days. You have to be working at blinding speed. *Au contraire,* my little screw-up. In the world we live in, "on time" is a quaint little phrase that means it is time to check out how I deal with missing a deadline. So, missing a deadline or not being on time is the first deadly screw-up we will tackle.

The second screw-up on the docket is being on budget. What is a budget, anyway? Is it some arbitrary set of numbers used to torment us? I think so. And so do most of us who can't seem to stay within its bounds. For us, we say that coloring between the lines is just not creative. In fact, it is down right oppressive or, at the least, pretty darn anal. Isn't business supposed to be about generating the big idea? Well, budgets don't ever seem to enter the equation on that, do they? We will keep thinking that way. Our second part of the dynamic duo is not being on budget.

Now, before I go much further, it is important for you to know that each business blunder we discuss is not your everyday, garden variety screw-up. When I talk about not being on time or on budget, I am not talking about being a few minutes late or a few pennies off. We are talking about being as close to this as me trying to hit a Roger Clemens' fastball with my eyes closed. This is for screw-ups the size of the *Hindenburg*. We are talking about the whopper of all screw-ups. With that as a preamble, let me move on to the rest of the seven deadly business screw-ups.

Screwed-up Plans

The third area of business screw-ups is the flawed plan. This is not the brilliantly crafted, career-building plan that makes you a hero. We are now into the realm of plans so blatantly flawed, a kindergartener could see that they contained massive amounts of doo doo.

Plans are such a big part of business and screwed-up plans are even a bigger part of business. When you can get an "Idiots Guide to Business Plans," you know the world is pretty much chock full of worthless plans. They are either taking up space on an office shelf or, worse, someone is actually trying to implement this turkey. Didn't they know that turkeys can't fly? Neither can this plan.

This chapter takes us on a wild ride of plans so rank, they make a landfill smell good. You may have guessed that this chapter will contain references to our government as the standard-bearer of worthless plans. And you would be right. Even in a book devoted to business screw-ups, you do have to have some benchmarks.

Screwed-up Presentations

My fourth business screw-up is the classic presentation mess up. Come on, we have all been there. The projector won't fire up, the computer crashes or the room just goes dark. All of these technical glitches are not only possible, but within the world of the living screw-up, they are destined to happen.

But, this chapter is much more than dealing with some sort of demented audio-visual guy or mutant IT manager. That, in and of itself, wouldn't make for the classic screw-ups that legends are made of. Although, I did witness an audio-visual guy actually break down and cry in the middle of a presentation once.

No, this chapter deals not only with the typical technical malfunctions everyone deals with, but goes well beyond that into the human element. Yes, it is those presentations that you know from the moment you are seeing it, that it is one big train wreck waiting to happen. But you can't avert your eyes because this presentation may go down in the Hall of Fame of presentation screw-ups.

If presentations are a way you make your living, then this chapter should help you keep on trucking, no matter how sorry you are. Or, for that matter, how much you messed up. Not to give away the chapter, but think about how you might recover from a presentation to your biggest client where you inadvertently show a slide of a proposal to his rival for half the money you are trying to gouge him for. Not too pretty is it? But, with a little bit of wisdom, you can not only survive this type of misstep but actually turn it to your benefit. Are we good here, or what?

Bad Hire

Our fifth foul-up is the bad hire. Now, just about everyone has made a mistake in hiring. You may have underestimated the work load of the job or you overestimated the candidate's capacity to actually walk and chew gum at the same time. Regardless of the circumstances, you end up with a round peg in a square hole. Hey, it happens all the time. Things don't always work out. "Big deal," you say. Put them on probation and then fire their rear. How hard can it be?

In this scenario, we are not going to talk about your typical hiring mismatch. We aren't shopping at Filene's Basement in this chapter. We are going to discuss a hire so horribly wrong the entire company is either laughing at it (and you for doing it) or are paralyzed by fear over what this person might do.

This is like the scene in *Alien* where the alien-being shoots out of the person's stomach and begins to wreak havoc on the world. That can happen in any company and to you. So if you have hired some terminal loser, now what do you do? Don't worry, I will guide you. You can get out this one just like the other foul-ups.

Signing Screw-up

You signed something that you shouldn't have. That is business, right? Even in this electronic age, there is enough paper to choke a horse.

Who hasn't signed something they regret. It might be your marriage license for all I know. It might have been that traffic ticket when you were really going the speed limit. Or it might have been a school paper that your son put in front of you that ended up getting him out of school for the rest of the semester.

We have all made blunders in signing things we shouldn't have. Seriously, who has actually read their mortgage agreement? You could be dead by the time you finished that one. The purpose of this chapter isn't to tell you to be more careful or to hire a lawyer to review every document you get. This is a chapter devoted to the ramifications of having your name on something that is so stupid your dog wouldn't have put his paw print on it. When you have your "John Hancock" on that, you may go down in history just like he did, but it will be the *Mad* magazine version of the Declaration.

So, if you have signed something you shouldn't have or have done some piece of correspondence that is so vile, insipid or just plain dumb, please read this chapter. You will be surprised to find that no matter how boneheaded you are, I can help you through it.

The Company Party

The previous seven deadly business sins are acts of ineptitude. I am assuming that if you are reading this book, you fall into the bottom half of the food chain. That seems to be where the most screw-ups reside. Of course, there are a number of top 10%er's who get too big for their britches and they pull a serious screw-up and end up with the rest of us. Those bright boys at Enron might fall into this category.

However, my last chapter has nothing to do with lacking the wherewithall to actually perform your job. This chapter is devoted to the mother of all screw-ups, the Company Party.

Other business screw-ups are peanuts compared to screwing up at the office party. When it is a Christmas party, it takes on an even more spiritual meaning. You may be able to deflect a bad presentation or hide a bogus budget, but there is little escape from being singled out at the office party as a loser.

The company party screw-up becomes the stuff of legends. Sitcoms are written about it. Movies are made of them. Why, even Las Vegas has a line on how many people lose it at the company party. I always bet on the over myself. I am rarely disappointed.

So, if you have just dunked yourself in the punch bowl at the company party or you find yourself in a compromising position in a closet with the intern, then this chapter is a must-read for you. Frankly, I am thinking of making this chapter into an ongoing podcast so you can download this puppy right at the party when your debauchery has taken place. At the very least, you should cut this chapter out of the book and tape it to the inside of your shirt for easy reference once the games begin.

So, there you have it. These are the seven deadly business sins that we will not only solve, but we will boldly take you where no loser has gone before. That would be back to his or her job with some shred of dignity after making what could be the screw-up of their business life.

I know that this is a pretty bold statement. And if I wasn't confident that I had the wisest of friends, I wouldn't offer it. But as you will see, if you follow along the logic train of the rest of the book, you won't get hit by that onrushing boss ready to paint you with so many pink slips you will look like a bottle of Pepto Bismol.

Chapter 3

What to do, now that you've screwed-up.

Ok, you've screwed-up. This isn't some low-grade foul-up. You have screwed-up big time, my friend, so let's talk about what to do. There are a number of options at your disposal. Some are actually the disposal of you, your co-workers or your job itself. But let's not get too far ahead of ourselves. There are some basic methods that have been proven effective in dealing with the screw-up.

Now the trick is the pick the right method for the right screw-up. Let's face it, if you don't pick the right way to deal with your massive screw-up, then you have screwed-up the screw-up. That is the double whammy. We can't stand for that. So, let me introduce you to a major icon that you will be seeing in this book. The Weasel of Wisdom.

Yes, you will have to be a bit of a weasel at times to retain your job and to maintain your dignity. While being a weasel isn't the greatest thing on earth, it does beat being an unemployed and downtrodden beaver. With all those big teeth, is it any wonder that the beaver unemployment rate is very high? But, I digress. You will see the weasel in subsequent chapters giving his or her opinion (take your pick) on what is the best path to take for each major screw-up.

Want to have fun? You can type in your own personal screw-up at www.youvescrewedup.com and the lovely weasel will give you his take on your plight. Unfortunately, if you are really using the website to deal with a major screw-up that is, in and of itself, a screw-up. It is too late. So, continue reading the book and learn, oh screwed one.

Here are the six proven methods to success in dealing with the screw-up. Remember, one size does not fit all and you cannot mix and match methods to screw-ups and get the same result.

1. Come Clean with it

The first method is pretty obvious but takes courage. You need to just come clean with it. Hey, it worked for George Washington in that cherry tree episode. He did pretty well with it. Of course, just about any book, article, talk show or counselor will tell you that you should fess up and admit your mistake. It is the best thing to do in any circumstance. Be a man, or woman, and admit that mistake. Praise will rain down on you from on high. Yeah, right.

Of course, those guys didn't send the company's payroll to a mystery account in Bangladesh. Now, the entire company isn't getting paid, including your boss, who has three ex-wives to support. Now, don't tell me that "coming clean" is the top method to deal with this screw-up. While coming clean is encouraged, remember that our goal isn't to report to our Sunday school class. It is to keep your job and then, if possible, keep your dignity. Sundays may have to wait. Put something extra in the plate.

2. Ignore it

Huh? Did it really happen? I just don't remember. Ignoring that screw-up or pretending that it didn't really happen can be an effective means of dealing with it. The old head-in-the-sand method can be a good one. It has worked well for ostriches for years. You don't mess with them, do you? Again, this method can be effective but it all depends upon the screw-up.

If you've just torched your house because you didn't have enough willpower to not smoke in bed, then it might be a bit hard to ignore your family as you sit and admire the rubble that used to be your home.

On the other hand, if you happen to be an unorganized person (or organizationally challenged) and lose an invoice (like the same one for every month of the year), will anyone ever really notice it? You might be able to ignore that sucker for years before it could come back and bite you. Hopefully, by then you have moved onto other greener pastures and have used other methods to more decisively deal with screw-ups.

3. Make an Excuse

Now you are getting aggressive. Make an excuse. Hey, I just had too much to do. I was stressed because we are just not reaching World Peace. Ok, that may not work for any problem, but you get the idea. When a screw-up happens and the finger comes pointing your way, make an excuse.

This is as old as "the dog ate my homework." It is easy to make an excuse but not as easy to find a credible one. That is the problem with the excuse. Just like "the dog ate my homework," that dog won't always hunt. For every one great excuse, there are a million lame excuses that might as drive you back to just coming clean.

The trick to the excuse is to have it outweigh your screw-up. You need to come off as much more screwed-up than the screw-up that you just committed. Whew!! But the excuse can be very effective. For example, if you didn't hit the right launch sequence on the missile because you were too busy fighting off three terrorists trying to steal the State Department secrets, well I think that you might get the benefit of the doubt. However, if you happened to spill mustard on your pants and as a result, the missile just whizzed into downtown Cleveland, then you might be facing the need for more than an excuse.

4. Blame it on Someone Else

It wasn't me. It was all their fault. "Mommy, Billy is picking on me." Don't you hate those kids? Who doesn't hate them? And you really hate them when they get away with it. Particularly after your sister has just tortured you and, in one final gesture of stupidity, you hit her in the arm. Then the cry goes up to mom and you are spending the next six months cleaning little tiles on the kitchen floor.

The old blame game. Honestly, work isn't much more advanced than kindergarten. There is always someone to blame and someone who is more than willing to throw that blame your way. And why do they do this? Because it works. It worked for your little sister at home and it can work in the workplace, too.

Imagine that you just took a hundred dollars out of the collection plate at church. Quick on your feet, you point to the minister (rabbi, pontiff, priest take your pick) and say, "His sermon drove me to do this crazy thing." Not a lot of credibility there, huh? Not much street cred, as they say in the hood. The blame game is only as good as the credibility or lack thereof of the person you are blaming it on.

You must pick your friends and mate wisely. But that is merely a warm-up act for picking the right person to blame. It must be so locked down, air-tight that everyone around you says, "Yeah, that's right." So, while blaming someone else can be very effective, it does come with its own set of rules.

5. Deny It Vehemently

"I did not have sexual relations with that woman," exclaimed former President Bill Clinton when confronted with the Monica Lewinsky affair. Wait a minute. I thought that it was pretty clear that you had an affair with this little tramp.
"Oh, when I refer to sex, I was referring to sexual intercourse. I clearly did not have sexual intercourse with this woman."
But you did have a sexual relationship with her. Right?
"Yes, but I did not have sex with her."
Huh?

See the power in the vehement denial. The key to this strategy is to be so bold and vehement about it, that it throws everyone for a loop. Bill Clinton was a master at this and many other things. Perhaps, every politician worth their intern is as well. When used right, the denial is classic.

I frankly think that the more farfetched it is, the better. A classic example of the denial is on an old episode of *Seinfeld* where George is at a girlfriend's birthday party and smells smoke in the apartment. He comes storming out of the apartment, knocking down kids, a clown and an elderly grandmother. As he is confronted on this by his girlfriend, he vehemently denies any wrongdoing. He says something like, "What may have looked like shoving to you was merely an attempt by me to get everyone close to the ground. When you have a fire, everyone should get close to the ground. Am I right?" You should be praising me for helping save lives rather than chastising me as some kind of coward."

Now that is one bold, audacious denial. *Seinfeld's* George was a classic in doing the denial. So, the denial can be a good defense once the screw-up happens. The bolder the denial, the better it will be. You can't go small here. You have got to be prepared to tell the fish story of all fish stories. Plus, it helps to have gone to a super-weasel law school.

The problem with the denial is that, just like the Clinton example, you can easily become a parody. Who really wants their legacy to be a denial quote? And as cool as that might be to some, it is not a real career enhancer. Again, in certain cases, the denial becomes a great gambit.

6. Simply Quit

Quitters never win and winners never quit. Ok, but quitters never get fired or taken to court for some ungodly screw-up, either. Quitting is the last resort. But, just like filing for bankruptcy, a quick quit, leaves you to fight another day.

In fact, if you get the weasel going, he can help you turn your quit into a heroic act. "Hey, that place was just so screwed-up, I felt compelled to quit." Of course, what you didn't say is that place was so screwed-up because you screwed them up. Oh, details, details.

Quitting is a bolder version of the vehement denial. It leaves people with their mouths agog. Just like hooking a big bass. Man, you can drop some jaws with "the quit." We are not talking about giving two weeks notice or wrapping up all your projects here. We are talking about an "I quit" and promptly walking out the door. Forget about that severance pay. That is the least of your problems, if you have had a screw-up big enough to quit over.

Hey, some screw-ups are that monumental. If a football coach gets beat 100 to 0, then he should quit. It is obvious that his players either are so pathetic or just quit on him. In fact, the coaching arena is filled with quitters. Kind of an ironic twist isn't it, the whole sports analogy about quitters not winning really isn't true. These coaches who get caught in a recruiting scandal or two, just quit and go to another sorry school to mess them up. Student-athletes, my rear. But, college athletics is a whole another screw-up to discuss in a later book.

So, let's get back to quitting. It ain't pretty but in certain instances, it is the best play to call. There, I finished on the sports metaphor.

So, now you have the magic answers to screwing up. Just to repeat the strategies; unless you screwed-up and forgot what you just read.

1. Come clean with it
2. Ignore it
3. Make an excuse
4. Blame it on someone else
5. Deny it vehemently
6. Simply Quit

That is my super-six screw-up strategies for success. I really didn't think I could get many S's in one sentence. Now, you are armed and ready to screw-up. The next chapters will be devoted to how to apply these strategies to business screw-ups. Watch for the weasel tips. He will tell you the most effective way to maintain your job and dignity after a major screw-up.

Chapter 4

The Budget Screw-up

Everyone has probably messed up on budgeting. There is likely to be an error in your checkbook or an unchecked spreadsheet in your past. In this chapter, we are not talking about the garden variety plus or minus 5% mistake. We are talking the huge budget screw-up.

Let me give you an example from my sordid past in advertising. I worked with a creative director who was notorious for basically ignoring any budget guidelines. He once did an annual report for a financial institution that was so far over budget that the bank's advertising director said, "Ron, I gave you an unlimited budget and you exceeded it." Now that is the type and magnitude of a budget screw-up that I am talking about.

It is so glaring that you will have to wear sunglasses to dim the lights that will be cast upon it. As with my compadre, Ron, you might go down in infamy over your basic disregard for fiscal responsibility. Or you just might go down, period.

Ok, so you've done it. You've screwed-up this budget so much that it is bigger than the Alaskan Highway project. What do you do? Let's take a look at your sinful six strategies and see what best fits. Also, be on the lookout for the weasel words of wisdom in the sidebars. If you are currently madly looking for a quick fix to your fiscal fiasco, you might look to the weasel. Otherwise, if you have time to mull over your options, then the problem may be bigger than the both of us.

Come clean with it

Regardless, let's look at the alternatives as we size up your problem. Frankly, I think that this is a problem that will be difficult to just come clean on. You don't just waltz into your boss and say, "Hey, you know that budget of $10 million you gave me to build out our IT infrastructure, well, I decided that I would spend $100 million and build a nuclear power plant."

This is not a cherry tree that you have chopped down. This is a fiscal fiasco of biblical proportions. So, just coming clean is likely not to be the solution for you.

Ignore it

Can you just ignore this type of problem? It all depends on the billing cycle. If your screw-up covers a couple of fiscal years and is prorated over a large amount of months, it might be possible to survive with the ostrich strategy. However, this problem involves money and documentation. That is a deadly combination for the ignoring strategy.

Make an Excuse

Sooner or later, there will be a reckoning on this little matter. So, while the ignoring strategy may be a nice short-term solution, it is likely to blow up in your fiscal fanny if you don't take other steps.

One step to take is to make an excuse. This can't be a lame excuse like, "I was never very good with numbers" or "my girlfriend left me so I became disoriented." With money involved, you can't take the sympathy route. I don't care if your house burned down, your wife ran off with the mailman and your kids are all social misfits. You've just cost me hundreds of millions of dollars. I might be sympathetic in that plus or minus 5% mistake world but now you have entered the zero tolerance zone.

You can go on the offensive with the excuse. For example, "You asked that I build a state-of-the-art IT system so I did. We needed it and that pittance for a budget wasn't going to cut it so here is the baddest IT system ever designed." It is a bold move. Most business objectives don't ever mesh up with the budgets anyway. I mean, when did you ever have the proper amount of money to do it right? So, this time you did it right! Right on! No one ever does it right, they usually do the best they can within the means that were given to them. But you, you went for it. Who can fault you for wanting to do the best possible thing, right?!

No one expects you to do the right job for the money at hand.

Blame it on someone

So, the twisted excuse is a possible solution to your problem. But is it the only or the best solution? How about doing the blame game? Goodness knows, with the screw-up that you have made, there is enough blame to go around the entire company and all of its alumni for the past 100 years.

This is not one where you can lightly say, "Gosh, Bob, when you said that the budget was $10 million, I took that to mean $10 million per week." This screw-up is beyond the simple misunderstanding. If you really want to place blame on someone, you must find something so incredible that it is beyond reproach.

Here is an example of what can work, "I had this project nailed except that the Boffo Corporation ran out of routers. That forced me to go to Doozy routers which forced me to scrap the entire system and retrofit the project to meet the deadline." This type of thinking is good on a number of fronts. First you blame another company and, if it is like most vendors, they have sorry products and equally sorry service. So, you get a few heads nodding when you start in about how worthless the Boffo Corporation is. Secondly, you throw out some technical babble that is tough to decipher. Heads are now nodding and thinking about the ramifications of not having this crucial part. Third, and this is the clincher, is that you blame it on the deadline. So, you've got the trifecta. You have a worthless vendor, some techno babble and an unreasonable deadline. Good work. You might keep your job and your dignity.

Vehemently Deny it or Quit

Your other two alternatives are to vehemently deny that it happened or to quit. Let's take the latter. You did screw-up and cost the company millions of dollars. If you are in the top 5% of all fiscal fiascos, you may have forced a bankruptcy. But, it is only money. This is no reason to storm in and quit. This has nothing to do with personal integrity. It is all about competence or lack thereof in your case. So, don't quit. Save that for some of our other screw-ups.

Don't be afraid of bankruptcy. It is a tool and not a condition.

This is also a tough one to vehemently deny. I know if Clinton can deny he had sex when he did, why can't you deny that you screwed-up the budget? Unfortunately, there is no grey area when it comes to money. The denial of "I did not go over budget," meaning the budget of Microsoft, is just not going to fly. You can try to say that it is pesos, but while you may be ready to have the bluster, you will likely not have the bullshit to carry this one off.

Vendors will help you to help them feather their nests.

Before I totally eliminate the denial route, there is a way to do the denial but it requires a weasel graduate degree. If you were this smart, you likely wouldn't have made such a blunder. But, there could be that one reader who could miraculously fall into this camp, so here it is. It requires a weasel for a vendor. That is the easy part. Again, most vendors are weasels so that is our operating assumption for project re-bill. You call the vendor and say that you need to have them bill their enormous bill in bite-size parts. Take that candy bar and make M&M's out of it. Then have them bill it to various jobs and people in the company. That way your project is clean. Or it may still be over budget but not in the gargantuan stage. Vendors do strange invoicing all the time and if you promise the vendor even more business, they will do your bidding for you. After you have given them the budget of a lifetime, they will have no reason to not help you. So, their bills are popping up on everyone's projects. Although surprise may reign, most people will end up sending them to accounting for payment. I call this the "let accounting deal with the mess" syndrome. So, there it is. You can lay out your denial loud and proud knowing that your project will be reasonably on budget. Now, that rest of the company, well, that is their problem.

So, the winner of round one goes to blame it on another inept corporation. That is the most likely way to retain your job and to keep your dignity. Congratulations. You have survived a budget screw-up. Would you like to try for something else? Let's move on to the next screw-up, shall we?

Chapter 5

The Deadline Screw-up

You've probably missed a deadline or two in your life. Most of us do. If you are like me, you probably are a serial deadline misser. I started missing deadlines as soon as there were deadlines to miss. From grade school on, I was missing deadlines like there was no *mañana*. Unfortunately, there wasn't a mañana with those nasty teachers.

I think that this training is solid preparation for on-the-job deadline missing. If you can miss a due date for turning in a term paper, it is pretty easy to not get a business report on time. So, like you, the missed deadline is almost an ingrained condition with me. Just ask the publisher about getting this puppy completed. Can you say, "missed another one?"

So, the missed deadline is about as common as a missed putt in golf. Usually, they both end in a similar fashion. At first, there is a lot of swearing, but afterwards you move on to another hole just like you move on to another project. In fact, after a while, it is an expected behavior.

Mother of all Missed Deadlines

What we are talking about in this chapter is not your everyday missed deadlines. You can and have dealt with that for years and lived for another day. What we are talking about here is missed deadlines that redefines the term missed deadline.

Let me give you an example of a friend of mine who was the supervisor of a construction crew in the rebuilding of Iraq. One of his workers (I use this term loosely) was granted a week's leave to spend his tax-free money in a vice-laden spree across Southeast Asia. (Now, you know why men actually work in these remote outposts. Hint: It isn't for the free meals.) Weeks turned into months and he didn't return. Nor did he write, call or send for his things. So, the supervisor called his parents and told them that it was likely that he was dead. Nine months later, this ding dong comes staggering back to work. He was amazed and rather indignant that his job was now someone else's (actually, it was given to a guy from Somalia who worked for half price). Now, that is a missed deadline.

Perhaps a more serious missed deadline might go something like this:

"Countdown; 3, 2, 1 ignition"
"Ah, Fred, didn't you put that fuse in the rocket?!"
"What are we going to tell the President and the rest of the world, Fred?"

Now, not putting the proper fuse in the space shuttle mission on time might get some folks a bit testy. That is one missed deadline of epic proportions.

My favorite business missed deadline is the old "didn't get the check in the bank on time so we missed our payroll" gambit. This is always a good one when you are dealing with thousands of irate employees and their equally irate families who are now pounding on your door to have you pay their mortgage bills.

That is the kind of deadline missing we are talking about here. We are talking big, hairy, audacious missed deadlines. This can be a case of you missing by a mile or nine months as the case may be. Or it might be a miss where the alarms are sounding like you just touched one of those obnoxious car alarms, only it was going off over your head with arrows pointing at you.

If this is happening to you, read on but do so quickly because time is a wasting. Or look for the quick answer from the weasel because he may be the only friend that you have right now.

Come Clean With It

Yeah, right. Come clean with it. This may be tough to say, "Hey, I know that I missed the deadline by nine months but I overslept." No, my friend, you are too late to come clean. Perhaps, had you warned someone eons ago, you wouldn't be in this mess in the first place.

Coming clean is not only wrong for this screw-up but really there is nothing to come clean about. This is not something someone may find out about later. This is later. It is much later as a matter of fact. So, we are just going to have to find a weasel way out of this one.

Ignore it

Could this be like the dream episode of television primetime soap opera, *Dallas*, where the entire year was just a dream? Perhaps, it could. Although, that dream year on *Dallas* really ticked me off. I wasted a year believing a story that turned out to be a dream. Man, I felt about as dumb as you might right now trying to find a nugget to save your rear since you missed a deadline.

If you are nine months late, perhaps they will forget about the deadline just like you did. It could be worth a try. Depending upon the deadline you have missed, ignoring it just might work. The key is what the weasel says on this one, "There are few hard deadlines." So, for those deadlines where there really isn't a true deadline, ignoring the deadline might be a good play for you.

Most deadlines have padding. Use it.

But, ignoring the outcome is not good if you are in the midst of missing a deadline that is one of those dreaded mission-critical deadlines. If you have a job where you are responsible for a mission-critical deadline, I really hope that you aren't reading this book. I really don't want some irresponsible bozo in charge of the flight deck or with their finger on the button of a nuclear bomb.

No book is going to help you if you are in those types of positions. But, dealing with a hard deadline where there is less weasel room is why we are in this business. It is to make you survive.

Make An Excuse

This is one where a note from your doctor may not cut it. However, a well-crafted excuse could be effective in this situation. Let's take a look at a missed deadline that is business threatening, but not life threatening.

Your boss has a big analyst meeting in the morning and is counting on you to show up and have all those well-crafted facts ready to baffle the analysts for another quarter while your boss looks for the next company to hi-jack. But, you don't show for the meeting. The boss is exposed like the emperor with no clothes. In this case, he is the emperor with no clue.

Obviously, a clueless, pissed-off boss is not to be taken lightly. Here is where a well-crafted excuse comes into play. The excuse you give him is this, "I missed the analyst meeting today because when going over the numbers last night, I found something that might have gotten us in trouble with the SEC. So, I stayed away in time for us to regroup. I'm sorry that you took a beating."

While your boss may have egg on his face, it is better than having an inmate named Bubba on his "you know what!" The lesson here is that if you can offer up a bigger catastrophe than the one you just committed, you just might get off with your job and your dignity.

Blame it on someone else

Can you blame someone else for missing a deadline? The answer is a resounding, "yes"! The most likely culprit is the twit that set this unreasonable deadline in the first place. I mean really, given your lack of competence, what was this guy thinking?

One key weasel tip everyone knows is that most deadlines are unreasonable. That fun fact can get you out of a pickle big time. You will get tons of people to side with you over an unreasonable deadline.

32   You've Screwed Up. Now What?!

All deadlines are unreasonable. Blame the deadline demagogue.

"Can you believe he asked me to develop an entire strategic plan in a day!?" you ask incredulously. The more incredulous you are, the better the blame will be diverted to its rightful owner, that dastardly deadline demagogue. Nice use of D's, huh!

Meeting a deadline usually requires sacrificing time or quality."

Blaming the deadline demagogue is a much better strategy than blaming someone else for not getting it done. You start at the root of the problem, with the originator of the request. Garbage in and constipation is what I say. It is hard to get the garbage out if you don't have time to get it in, in the first place.

Now, if there is someone in your office that is a bigger bonehead than you, then you can play the traditional blame game. Again, only try this when you are positive that the associate in question is a total loser. And that you, even in your weakened state, are still light years ahead of him.

There is one person in every company who is always missing a deadline. Get to know them.

"Hey, Ralph was doing the calculations for that project," you say remorsefully. Heads nod and eyes roll as your colleagues and your boss understand. Ralph is a total loser and the project was doomed from the start. Case closed. You have dodged another one. You must make sure Ralph continues to stay employed so you can stay employed, because, without that pincushion, you are sunk.

Deny it vehemently

You can review the previous chapter to understand how to weasel out here. You can deny aspects of the deadline and make a convincing courtroom case. But, the denial path is littered with fallen executives. Don't be one yourself.

In this case, the denial has to be air tight. Look to the weasel for some help on this one. Remember that deadlines are always changing. You may have been working right away on the original deadline and then the client decided to accelerate the date by a week or two. Oops.

Deadlines constantly change. Capitalize on it.

With the stopping and starting of projects and deadlines, it is easy to deny you may have missed this one. The key to the deadline denial is to have great indignation.

"You think I missed the deadline. With the way this deadline changes, I have probably missed 10 of them by now," you say with great indignation.

You have just completed a brilliant denial. The beauty of this denial is that you admit you missed the deadline, but you redirect the effort to the bouncing ball of deadlines.

Quit

Missing a deadline is nothing to quit over. You screwed-up, but it isn't like you committed a crime, is it? With all those ways to get past the deadline screw-up, you can miss deadlines for years without even blinking an eye.

So, remember that all deadlines are unreasonable. Even the best deadlines usually have padding. Deadlines are constantly changing. But most importantly is that deadlines are an arbitrary artifact of daily life. Hey, what are a few missed deadlines among friends anyway.

Ignore, blame it on the deadline demagogue, deny it or find something or someone worse than this mistake and move on. Speaking of, let's move on to the next chapter. Tomorrow is fine. We are on no deadline here.

Chapter 6

The Presentation Screw-up

I can see those throats tighten up, those hands get clammy and the stomachs doing flip flops. It is presentation screw-up time. And who hasn't had their share of presentation screw-ups? Show of hands, please. I thought so. We've all been there. The spotlight hits you and you act like a deer in the headlights. Freezing up, stammering, simply goofing up is pretty common fair for presentations. Even the greatest presenters make a mistake now and then.

What we are going to discuss here are those classic presentation screw-ups. These are screw-ups that become urban myths and legends. They take on a life of their own and become a part of corporate folklore. You don't want to go down in some perverse corporate fairy tale so read on.

Fortunately, I have seen and been involved in hundreds of presentations so the opportunity to see from the screw-up masters is great. One classic presentation that has gone down in corporate folklore was for an aircraft company's advertising account. Our team was poised, prepared, and presentation ready. The only problem was the slide show was a key element of our presentation. This presentation was in the day of yore, long before Powerpoint dominated the landscape. In this era, companies used slides as one of their main screw-up forms.

In this case, we had crafted a multi-slide show using five projectors that had an aircraft going across five screens along with the client's name. Big stuff. Too bad that the slide trays didn't have their lids on and that when the audio-visual guy got it rolling; slides were popping like Orville Redenbacher's popcorn. After much swearing and consternation, the slides got back in their trays for a second run at it and they were all upside down. Needless to say, there was no third attempt and there was a new audio-visual guy the next day.

Murphy's Law of presenting is that some Audio/Visual thing will screw-up.

There are lots of cases of equipment foul-ups, power failures, disks not having the presentation and other presentation maladies. Then there are the confrontation presentations where your well-crafted point of view spins wildly out of control.

One such example was a presentation for an English Toffee candy bar where we proposed using an English type as a spokesperson. Seems pretty safe, doesn't it? English candy bar and English guy seem to go together. But, the President of the candy company said that he didn't want to be known as an English candy. This was America, damn it.

So, our President's retort to him was, "Then why did you print English toffee on the label?" But, at least the slides worked well for this one.

Or how about the presentation where we used a bulldog as a demonstration of ruggedness, only to find out that the prospect was allergic to dog hair. As soon as he got within five feet of that dog, he puffed up like a balloon. But, the PowerPoint was great.

You get the picture or maybe in the case of a screwed-up presentation, you really didn't get it. Now that you have been involved in one of those classic screw-ups, how do you handle it?

Come Clean

I know that you thought that I would never recommend coming clean with it. But, here is a case where coming clean works. Everyone fears presenting and most people, unless they are just heartless bastards, will empathize with you.

Everybody fears presenting so there is lots of empathy for presentation mistakes.

In the case of the aircraft presentation, with a lot of groveling, we actually got the account even though we had one of the all-time worst presentations known to mankind. Our President called the aircraft big dog the next day and said, "That was the worst presentation that I have ever been a part of. Don't judge us on that one event, look at all the great work we have done. We are the best fit for your business." I can't go into all the other groveling and concessions that were given. The bottom-line is, by coming clean, we got another chance.

In fact, if you come clean with gusto, you will offset that bumbling presentation you just royally screwed-up.

Ignore It

When you are a deer in the headlights, there is nothing more you would like to do than to have everyone ignore you. But, unfortunately, once you are on stage, it's tough to change the channel. They need to develop a TIVO for presentations that will record the presentation so you can skip or edit out all the screw-ups. Until that happens, ignoring it really isn't an option.

In fact, the more you ignore it, the more clueless you look. This is not one of those things that can be hidden somewhere in the fine print. Your ass is on the line, exposed to the world. And it ain't pretty.

Unless you want to go down as a presentation screw-up and clueless to boot, don't try to brush this one under the carpet. That dirty underwear is out there in plain view.

Blame it on someone else

Look no further than to the wisdom of the weasel for pinning blame on someone. That someone is the IT guy or you're A/V guy. Take your pick. They usually suck. Everyone knows they suck. And with that kernel of wisdom, it is easy to pin the blame on them and get a lot of nodding heads.

Everyone knows that A/V or IT people are worthless.

"That damn A/V guy screwed me again," is a phrase heard every day in every office and conference room around the globe. In fact, it is probably a more international phrase that "CFO's are all slippery eels," which they are by the way. But that is another chapter.

If your presentation screw-up is in any way related to poor audio-video planning or any technical malfunction, you have a built in scapegoat. Now, don't you feel more confident for your next presentation?

If your screw-up was content related, then it gets a bit trickier. If you were in charge of writing the presentation yourself, there is your out. Who in their right mind would trust someone as lame as you to write a presentation of any magnitude?

In this case, you can blame it on an inept organization that should have better checks and balances. I mean, you should be getting some help now, shouldn't you? You can't shoulder this load by yourself and carry on a creditable presentation, now, can you?

By the way, these are all rhetorical questions and ones that you can surface as the blame goes round and round.

So, you can easily blame it on an inadequate process. Trust the weasel. Almost all organizations have pathetic checks and balances. Do you really think people have time to check others work or thoughts? Not in this day and age.

No organization has a good check and balances system for presentations.

If you get bold and know there is some pathetic loser, even bigger than you, that you can blame it on, feel free to give it a go. However, presentation blame is not the same as deadline blame. It is much more personal so don't single out the pathetic loser until you have exhausted the rest of your weasel opportunities.

Deny It

I did not inhale that marijuana cigarette," said former President Bill Clinton. Can that guy weasel or what? He is my role model weasel. I guess if you can deny that you smoked the evil weed because you may have puffed but didn't suck it down, then denying anything is possible.

But, in the case of presentation screw-ups, denial is a tough nut to crack. Unlike Wild Bill, everyone that is anyone saw this train wreck. Even if you get bold enough to deny that a certain aspect of the presentation wasn't bad, there is still the awful mess that needs to be picked up.

Can you imagine this dialogue after the presentation screw-up?

"Jim, I heard your PowerPoint presentation actually contained satanic symbols. And the prospect ran from the door to seek a priest."

"Bob, the content of the presentation was sound so I really don't understand your question."

Come on Jim. A good attempt at misdirection but once the PowerPoint pops, there is no putting it back in the projector. For god sakes, come clean on it before you go down the denial road. Believe me, it is a much stronger path to take.

Quit

No matter how big and how much you blundered on this presentation, it is nothing to quit over. And don't try for the sympathy vote of, "Man, this presentation stunk so bad, I might as well quit." It is a weak ploy and the worst thing that can happen is your boss might think that's a good idea and sack you.

The only time to even consider calling it a day is if this presentation means that you either have a job or don't. Sometimes if you are pitching an account, your job might be on the line. If the presentation is screwed, and you know that you are doomed, then you might consider quitting. But the only time to quit is in the presentation itself. This is a bold, bordering on maniacal, move but it can work. Hear me out on this one before you turn the page. If the presentation is screwed-up and you know it, but it isn't all your fault, then and only then, do you get up and tell the client that you will not be a part of something so lame and hope he recommends the company that will get his account call you for a job.

It is a pre-emptive strike on what you will lose anyway so it might be worth a shot. You do risk your integrity or what little amount of it that you have doing this, but if it is all about the almighty dollar, then this may be a good move for you.

However, for most of us, just let them fire you. Then benefits are a lot better than if you quit.

Just a parting shot on this chapter, presentations are made to be screwed-up so don't feel bad if you are one of the millions of business folks who really uncorked a major screw-up. This is one of those rare times in life where the truth can set you free. Coming clean with it is a good way to deal with the presentation *faux pas*. If this doesn't work, there is usually plenty of blame to go around so find a scapegoat and ride him until you can get a transfer.

Chapter 7

Screwed-up Plan

Have you ever woken up in the middle of the night drenched with sweat as you thought about the impending train wreck that was going to result as a part of your plan? If you have, this chapter is for you. And if you haven't, you are either brilliant, in which case, you really are slumming reading this book, or you are so far into denial that you can't see straight.

Regardless, the world is awash in screwed-up plans. Can you say, "Weapons of mass destruction"? President Bush's plan to clean Iraq of those nasty weapons of mass destruction was one screwed-up plan. It does, however, pale in comparison to Hitler's plan to rule the world. Oh, I forgot that the USA would kick my ass. And that same forgetfulness got the Japanese nuked. Talk about some poor planning.

Now we know that Washington D.C. is littered with screwed-up plans as are their international counterparts. We business types are much more disciplined than those pork-spreading politicians. Yeah, right?!

Let's me see. Does Enron come to mind? Now there was a plan to turn a nice utility into a hedge fund. Or WorldCom's plan to take over the telecom world, which ended in a bad patch of deceit and worthless broadband. One of my favorites is Coke's bold plan to change its formula to New Coke. Nevermind that one out of four Americans loved the original. You built one of the most revered brands on the planet and now you want to kill it. Now that is crazy.

Every day businesses crank out screwed-up plans and then blindly follow them like lemmings leaping off a bridge. Many of these plans don't have a chance from the get go. A Dilbert cartoon sums up a classic planning dilemma. In it, Dilbert tells his pointy headed boss, "I can't do a plan until you tell me the strategy."
The pointy headed boss replies, "My strategy is to make you do a plan."

So, there you have it. That is some perfect business logic. If you are now in the midst of a plan that has a big "S" on it, I can tell you right now, it doesn't stand for Superman. It stands for "Screwed-up." You are staring a one big train wreck. It might be a product that will fail. It may be a lawsuit waiting to happen. Or it might mean that your division may go into the crapper. Whatever the results are this demon plan will reek. You need to deal with it on your terms. So, let's look at the alternatives one more time.

Come Clean with it

"Guys, uh, I've been thinking. This plan is going to get us put in jail." Can you really come clean with a plan that is going down like a lead zeppelin? Not the most prudent thing to do. And our weasel is one prudent weasel.

Taking a page from the weasel, the one way you can come clean is to change the plan mid-course. Yes, the mid-course correction is the cornerstone of all good planning. As the weasel says, "Plans change all the time." You need to use this knowledge, my son.

All plans change.

If you are taking the plane down, one of the ways for you to deal with it is to pull up. Pulling up takes some nerve, but more importantly it takes speed. You need to come at the change so that no one questions the past or why this course you have set is going to have you falling off the edge of the earth.

There is nothing like a quick reaction to save the day. And that is what you are going to have to do. Pick an item out of the news and go with it. Come running in to your boss' office with the latest Daily News and say something like:

"My god, Bill, gas prices have just pushed over $3.00 a gallon. We must change our plan to react to the consumer carnage that will ensue."

This was not a random quote that I picked here. Always pick some industry that is perceived as being bad. I would say that the Oil Industry is pretty much up there on that note. Remember the *Valdez*? Exxon sure won't forget it. The oil industry is a pretty easy target on this one. And if that doesn't work, you can always fall back on the federal government.

Some outside force always changes a plan.

"That darned Fed raised interest rates again today. We need to scrap this plan and change course as soon as possible before the economy craters." That should do it. Plan screw-up averted and you are a hero. Yes, the weasel would be proud. But, there are other ways of dealing with the screwed-up plan, too. Read on.

Ignore It

Even if you wake up in a fit one night knowing that the well-intended plan you crafted is going to unravel like a sorry ball of yarn, there is the possibility of ignoring it. How, you may ask, can this be ignored?

If you are in a big company, the chances are pretty good that you will be moved around and the plan you created will be someone else's monster to slay. So, you can bury your head in the sand if you move to a new sand pile.

If you want to be proactive about things, (which is very much out of character for you) you may even request a transfer to another division. Hopefully, this division is so far away from your current job that you won't feel the nuclear fallout of your plan going down in flames.

Ignoring flaming plans is the hallmark of any Fortune 500 company and the government. The whole goal of these organizations is to develop cool plans. Whether they work or not is not really the point. It is the plan that is hero and not the result. So, if you are a part of such an entity, plan away and don't worry.

If, however, you are one of those unlucky sorts, who have a job with some sort of accountability, then read on. Ignoring the problem is the kiss of death for you.

Blame it on someone else

Where do we begin? There are so many people to blame on the flaming plan that there isn't room on the ark for all of them. Frankly, the blame game is almost like shooting fish in a barrel.

Let's start with the Board of Directors. Hey, they approved this turkey. Everyone knows that boards are basically well-paid lackeys. They are paid to be abused. So, start right in. When that fickle finger of fate points your way, play the board card. It is a slam dunk.

Maybe you go hunting with someone on the board so you don't want to lose your lease privileges. No problem, pick any of a million professional services groups who advise the company. Legal counsel is always an easy target. No one likes a lawyer. Just pick one who won't sue you if you blame them. Accountants are number jockeys waiting for blame. And the best of all are ad agencies or management consultants. Pin the tail on them. Their hinnies are so numb from being a pin cushion of blame, they won't mind.

Boards are typically bunglers.

Fun isn't this. Let's face it, no one in your organization should have trusted you to make a plan anyway. As it makes it way up the food chain, there are so many people to blame who should have seen your stinker. You just take your pick.

The only thing to remember in the blame game is to pick a target that needs future work. That is why any professional services group is great fodder. They won't come after you because they think once you leave this sinking ship, you will infect another company and need their services. The board is the same. They need those part-time gigs to get away from their wives so they will take a few bullets as long as there is another company they can "board up" on.

Make an Excuse

The best excuse for a failed plan is lack of execution. Just look at the NFL. Any coach worth his salt will say he developed the world's greatest game plan only to watch some dunderheaded offensive lineman jump offsides and ruin the play. Or it might be that the wide receiver smoked too much reefer the night before and forgot his pass route.

"Dude, man, I thought you were going to throw to my outside shoulder!"

"I did you pothead, you were looking between your legs."

So, when in doubt, the weasel says that no company is capable of executing a plan, particularly your company. Let's face it, if you are in charge of planning at your company do you really think that there are more capable people than you trying to carry this thing out?! Get real! If you are in a planning capacity, lord knows what idiots are out there on the front lines. This is a slam dunk. Everyone will know your plan is doomed from the start. So, crank up the plan of the century and use that to get out of this company.

All plans are poorly executed.

You are likely to get a great job somewhere else with this approach. Take a look at this plan. I wasted it on this company since they are all a bunch of dolts. Who can disagree?

If using the execution excuse isn't to you liking, the time-honored "not enough resources" or "not enough time" are the standbys. Again, what company ever properly funds a plan?

"Yes, you in the back looking like a weasel."

You say that no company ever properly funds a plan. Bingo! You would be correct. The same goes for not having enough time to get it done right. If someone says that the plan failed, all you have to do is say, "you won't say that a year from now." It hasn't had enough time. The time machine can literally buy you time until you have to use the "those idiots didn't execute it right even after I gave them a year to do it."

So, one excuse can beget another in this case. Planning is an infinite do-loop as is the excuse for not having a good plan.

Deny It

"Baker, are you responsible for this plan that is taking us down," screamed the pinheaded boss.

"Just what part of the plan are you referring to, sir?," you ask shrewdly.

"Why the part of the plan that has more red ink than a Holland Tulip Festival," he wails.

"I didn't pen that part of the plan, sir. That must be another department," you suggest and live for another day.

In this case, the denial is very Clintonesque. Once you make someone define parts of a plan or even a version of the plan, you are home free. Another way to handle the boss would be to say something like this:

"Are you referring to plan 3.1 or version 9.21, sir?", you ask smugly.

Once you suggest that the plan you may have crafted has gone through various stages of edits, re-writes and other nonsense, even the most ardent boss will know he has met his match. He has lost to the system of organizational incompetence. Every company with more than 20 employees goes through it. Plans must be done as a team, reviewed with various departments, re-written for management and so on. Heck, there is no telling who actually did the plan after a few months. And believe me, no one will be waving their hand in the air to take credit for this lame plan once they see that it is going nowhere.

Organizations make bad plans.

So, the denial can be a very easy weasel. Remember that no one owns a plan if it fails and everyone owns the plan if it succeeds. Now that is some true weasel wisdom.

Quit

Are you nuts?! Don't ever think about quitting over a screwed-up plan, unless you see parallels between your company and Enron. Then, by all means, leave now because that baby is going to explode like a nuclear holocaust.

The only other time to quit is if you feel that on paper your plan is so good that it might get you a better job than you deserve. If you feel that way, and with your track record that could be one faulty assumption, then go ahead and give your notice.

You know that there is a limited window of time between putting the plan to paper and when you will see the train wreck of the plan being implemented in your company. It is best to leave on a high note. Take that plan and go to the competition. Tell them that you have given the best plan of your life to these guys, but they don't know what to do with it.

You will have them eating out of your weasely little hand. Every company feels they can do it better than their competition. Use this knowledge, little one, to gain the big job. Otherwise, keep your job and don't look back.

Chapter 8

Company Party

Why do companies have parties? No one wants to be there. It is a big waste of money. All most employees think about is that if they didn't throw this lavish party, I might have had $100 for a bonus. I don't know about you, but I don't think that the company party ever increased shareholder value. But, on the plus side, it is one of the bigger business stages for huge personal screw-ups.

In fact, I think company parties were invented before television as a means to generate water cooler talk. This is probably how water cooler talk was in the 1940s.

"Hey, Fred, did you see Mr. Beasley cutting the rug with that intern? I bet Mrs. Beasley will be frosted when she hears about that."

And so goes another company party with company lore attached to it. Company parties are much like New Year's Eve parties. There are lots of rookies drinking and lots of attempts to have "meaningful" encounters. But with people who you work with day in and day out, you get an even more powerful combination. This is booze as "truth serum" effect. Somebody, perhaps you, will say something that everyone has thought for years, but either doesn't have the nerve or the adequate 401k plan to say. Here is an updated company party dialogue.

"Mr. B, I believe that you are called Mr. B because the "B" stands for butt-head. You are the most incompetent person in this god-forsaken company."

Now that should get the boss's attention, shouldn't it? So, between infidelity and popping off, the company party holds a treasure trove of screw-ups. Throw in poor social graces like spilling your wine on the boss's wife or having the salmon slide off the table into your pants and you have the earth, wind and fire of screw-ups.

Because company parties are begging for a screw-up, you just couldn't help yourself. I mean, it is your destiny to screw-up and this is one of the bigger corporate stages for a screw-up, so why not you. It actually demands that you do it.

So, you commit the mother of all office party screw-ups. You go for the trifecta. You molest the intern, pour wine on a co-worker and then take the mike and insult the boss. I guess the public browbeating of the boss, while you are holding the intern's bra in one hand and a bottle of wine in the other hand, will go down as a major screw-up. Congratulations, you are now a part of company folklore.

When they re-write corporate history, your name will be there on the infamous trifecta night at the company party. OK, perhaps you didn't do the trifecta, but you did any one of the myriad of other company party screw-ups. What do you do?

Come Clean With It

If you go to your boss and admit you screwed-up, he will say, "Duh!" You are now a part of company folklore. There is no need to come clean with it. Your laundry on this one is so dirty that there isn't a box of Tide or Clorox big enough that could get this puppy clean.

Any type of coming clean will beg for the reason why. So, a simple, "yes that was me molesting the intern and then hooking up a satellite transmission to tell the world what a dolt you are" may not generate the sympathy you may be seeking.

If you are expecting that your boss will forgive you on this one, you are more of a screw-up than I thought. If this is the case, you should immediately stop reading this book and seek either professional help or legal council. You are way out of my league.

Most employees wish they had the nerve to do what you did.

There is only one exception to this rule. If your screw-up was too much honesty, then confronting that could be a good thing. As the weasel says, "Most employees wish they would have said it." Of course, by having some restraint, they are still employed while you are reading a book trying to see if you can survive.

If you said something that was a classic *faux pas*, then coming clean is a route to go. If you said, "This Company really sucks because our products cause cancer," go with it. Tell the boss that while you may have come on strong, we really do have a problem here. He may still fire you but at least you go out with some dignity. But, there is a chance that he will know you are right and give you a promotion for having the nerve to take on the truth. Just make sure that whatever you said is the truth. We wouldn't want to come clean for anything less than the real deal.

So, in the case of the company party screw-up, typically coming clean just isn't going to cut it. Let's take a look at your other options.

Ignore it

I am afraid that it is too late to ignore this one, Bucky. Let's face it, if you have done this screw-up right, you may already have your own website or at least a page in the annals of the company's folklore on colorful incidents.

This is not like an accounting error that you can brush aside and hope that the company is too incompetent to catch. It is difficult to pretend that it didn't happen when people are building monuments to your audacity.

Here are some tips on when to know if you are well past the ignoring stage of this screw-up.

When a co-worker comes up to you and says, "Jim, I wish that I had the guts to tell the board what a crappy company this is. We are all behind you." There are two things to remember from this type of response. First is that everyone must have seen you blast the company. Second is that anyone who says they are behind you is so far behind you that you can't see them. You are on your own for this one.

Another tip is when a co-worker comes up to you and says, "Jim, we heard that you covered the intern with a chocolate mousse before you molested her. Awesome, man."

Again, you can assume from this response that first off, the entire company knows of your affair. Secondly, you had better be calling one tough trial lawyer because the lawsuits will be flying.

All of this is a long-winded way of saying you have already committed the mother of all screw-ups. Don't commit another one by trying to pretend that it didn't happen. Let's find you some action that can actually help you.

Blame it on someone else

Now we are talking. There are plenty of people to blame for your actions, least of all is you. Let's start with some easy ones and then go on to the more exotic ways to play the blame game.

As any weasel knows, "there is always a wanton intern or secretary in every office." That is a fact. If there is an office of more than five people, chances are great that someone wants to get in someone else's knickers. So use that fact. Blame it on them. Admit that you are weak and place the blame where it belongs, at the foot of some office trollop.

There is always an office skank or intern. Use them.

"Look boss, I am a weak man and the office bimbo made me do it. She even made me say bad things about you to divert attention from our sordid affair."

The fact is that if your boss is a man. He is probably so grateful that your weakness spared his weakness that he will say, "I know how temptation is and while I don't condone your behavior, I believe that you are basically a good man." Hopefully, he will say it better than that, but you get the gist of it. You have just skated by blaming the skank. It is as simple as that.

The office skank is pretty easy pickings for placing the blame. It is believable and is usually forgivable. Another person to blame is the office instigator. Just about every office has one. If you ever watch an episode of *Leave it to Beaver* on TV Land, check out Eddie Haskell. He is one major instigator. He will egg on Wally or the Beav to do his bidding and then sit back and laugh when it goes bad. There is an Eddie Haskell type in most offices. They are weasel wantabees. Except that no one really wants them.

There is always a loudmouth instigator in every company. Use them.

So, when confronted with an office party snafu, you can turn the blame to the office instigator.

"I didn't really think that your wife would like it if I gave her a power wedgie using the trout almandine, but Eddie said that it was a custom in her country."

The boss will immediately do the eye rolling thing when he hears the word "Eddie," or your equivalent of Eddie. He is likely to believe just about anything that big Ed suggests that you do. And because of who you are, he is also likely to believe that you are a lemming and will do anything that Eddie suggests. You may be an undignified lemming, but you are an employed lemming so don't gripe.

The secret to the blame game is to make sure that you get that eye rolling reaction. If the eye rolls then by all means, roll with it.

Make an Excuse

If you are a child of the 60s, 70s or 80s this should be a cakewalk for you. It is all about sex, drugs and rock n roll. Hey, you were horny, you lost control. It happens. You can't handle your liquor. It happens. You just got caught up in the music. Ok, maybe the best two out of three.

Of the big three that I mentioned, I would add the super biggie of "stress" to the list. This is a sure-fired one to fall back on. Everyone is stressed out and if the party is held at Christmas time, so much the better. I don't know of a soul that isn't stressed at Christmas. You just happened to snap, but so do lots of people. It is one of the peak times of suicide in the year. Of course, if you live in Buffalo, you take the whole art of suicide to another level.

Stress is high at the holidays. Everyone is ready to snap.

Fact is, people get stressed and then do crazy things to relieve that stress. Of course, most don't go to the extremes that you just did, but between the kids at home, the boss at work, the bills to pay and presents to wrap, you went a bit wacko. Most people can relate to being stressed out. It happens to the best of them.

Perhaps stress isn't your solution for an excuse. This could be particularly true if you are a slug and are just there trying to pick up a paycheck. Then the stress excuse may not cut it. I can see it now:

"Boss I am so sorry, but the stress of work and home just got to me. I snapped."

"Franklin, aren't you the guy who sleeps in the closet every day from 1 until 4pm? Why I've had to re-schedule the cleaning crew just to accommodate your naps. Now, what is this stress you're talking about?"

If you are like Franklin, then bypass stress and go for the gold with alcohol. "I just can't handle my booze." No kidding, we noticed that you were swinging from the chandelier with the intern's panties on your head.

Your old friend, alcohol can be your savior. In fact, you can even get aggressive with the alcohol excuse and turn it into a blame game. You can blame the company for serving alcohol in the first place. Really, don't they know that there are weak worthless sots like you that attend these things? They should pay you not to file a lawsuit. The emotional damage could ruin you for life. Not to mention what it might do to the intern.

Booze is a truth serum. Everybody forgives a drunk.

Yes, the too much booze card can come in very handy. It might even get you released from work to attend classes on dealing with your problem. You could ride this gravy train to pension city. Alcohol is the excuse that keeps on coming, like your stomach after too many vodka tonics.

Deny It

After learning about the alcohol excuse, it is tough to get into denial but it actually can be a fun gambit. Now, you can't deny that you actually did the full monte. But, you can certainly deny the intent of your actions.

Let me give you a classic example from an old *Seinfeld* episode. George trots into his boss's office and throws a fit and quits. The next day, he is back at work acting like nothing happened. When his boss confronts him about it, he says," Oh that, I was just playing. I didn't mean anything by it. Oh, you thought that I was serious. It was all an act."

That episode is worth renting to see denial in motion. George has it down pat. And you can too. You can't be any more of a loser than George. The trick to denial is to admit it but to change the perception. Let me demonstrate:

"Lola and I were just hamming it up. She gave me her bra just to get a rise out of everyone. I really can't believe that you fell for it."

The more incredulous you are, the better the denial.

"Geez, I can believe that Sam would think that I was a total drunk, but I thought that you knew me better than that."

Follow this up with a hurt puppy look and you have mastered denial. Depending upon your party *faux pas*, you can use denial. Done well, it can not only work but it can leave you better off than before. But it is all about practice. The denial is not for the amateur. You must practice your act and have it down before attempting to pull it off. Otherwise, a poor denial could have you looking for the final solution.

Quit

Party foul-ups typically end in a firing and not quitting. However, there is always a place for quitting. But, let's get real. Party goofing isn't like budget bungling. You may have embarrassed yourself, an intern, perhaps a co-worker and a boss, but it isn't like you burned down the place.

We really don't recommend quitting just because you did something embarrassing. Heck, this may be the first time people even noticed you. If you play this right, you might gain some notoriety. You are company folklore. You can't leave now. Your co-workers are already thinking about what act of debauchery you might try at next year's party. You are now an important member of the team.

The only way you should quit is if you feel that your boss is going to can you. Perhaps, the wife wedgie will drive him to do it. If not for the company, just to save face at home. If this is the case, then you might as well go for it. But don't go down quietly on this.

Heck, if you are folklore now due to the party, just imagine how you might be immortalized if you create an equally big scene while quitting.

So, go down swinging. Tell him that not only do you quit, but you will sue him for emotional duress. This moron drove you to do it so lay it on him. You might actually win a lawsuit. If he had the brains to hire you, he can't be too smart now, can he. The quit can be lucrative, but only once.

So, before you throw down the gauntlet, give the other ways to deal with this a try.

Chapter 9

The Hiring Screw-up

Just to take a flier, I would say the chances of your company making a bad hiring decision is more predictable than the sun rising. Let's face it, they did hire you. That should tell you something about their hiring standards. You and your company hire one loser after another. It is not unusual. Your company may subscribe to the pygmy philosophy of hiring. This says that if you continue to hire people less than yourself; pretty soon you will have a company filled with pygmies. Welcome to your world. It is a death spiral built with pygmy power.

However, while you may be a weak employee, you are likely to be a harmless one. Most company pygmies hide from work, and unlike their savage counterparts, they are typically not meat eaters. In fact, they are likely not being too aggressive at all. If you rolled up all your pimpled face pygmy people, they would make a nice bland wallpaper covering for the office. At least, then they would have a function.

Every company has these types of losers. You may be one. The guy who punches in and clocks out without anyone really knowing what he does. Being invisible is a good thing in a big company. When the world was full of pensions, it was the pygmy union that sought them. Sadly, now the pygmies are going the way of the three martini lunch. You must stand out from the crowd. 'Be brave or be gone' is the new motto.

This leads us to the type of bad hires I am talking about in this chapter. These are difference makers. But, they make a difference like an Ebola virus. This is a rampant, mutant employee running amuck in the halls of the company wreaking carnage wherever he or she goes. That paints a nice picture, doesn't it? Let me give you a few examples from my storied career, based on some totally screwed-up hires that I have witnessed, but have also survived.

The first example is the IT guy gone mad. In this case, we will call him Fred. Fred was a Vietnam vet who still was behind the wheel of a gunboat going up the Mekong Delta. He was the only guy that saluted people in an advertising agency. And I am not talking about a single-fingered salute (since that is quite common in an advertising agency) but a military salute and "Sir, yes sir." Yes, Fred was unique but ad folks don't know much about IT so we all thought it was maybe the way it should be. Boy were we ever wrong. Fred, in a veteran haze, locked down the entire computer system to exorcise all Mac files that were crowding space on his server. Fred believed all Macs were evil. Too bad those Mac files contained the ads that were going to clients that day and for many days to come. Then, Fred wrote a manifesto that he sent to all employees and clients regarding the sorry state of affairs at the agency. All in all, Fred about cratered the agency within the two months that he was there. Now, that is a mutant hire.

However Fred, while manic, was nothing compared to John, our heroin-addicted creative director. John would shoot up daily, usually in a darkened conference room but sometimes the urge was so great that he would slide under his desk in his cubicle and jam a needle in his rear. It got so bad that none of the cleaning people would go near his cubicle for fear of getting a bloody needle poking them from the trash.

John was not a happy addict and an even less happy creative guy. This was especially true when someone challenged his copy. In one episode, he cursed the account person and then threw his typewriter (for those of you under 40, this is a machine that looks like a computer but without all the memory) out the window of an eight-story downtown building onto the street below. Fortunately, no one was hurt. I can't say the same for the time when he threw a different account executive over his cubicle wall. Unfortunately, the account guy bounced on his head and was out like a light. He is now retired after a rather nice settlement over a "wrongful throwing" lawsuit that he won against the company.

Even with this mayhem, John survived because clients thought he was creative. This shows that clients don't know the difference between a savant and a savage. John's undoing came at the hands of a client who he happened to slip LSD to at a television shoot. John thought this was a welcoming gesture to his world. Turns out he was wrong. The client had a flying delusion and almost dove out the balcony of his penthouse hotel room. Some quick thinking by yet another account executive saved him from certain doom. The doom was saved for John, who today is at a halfway house writing the daily soup menu.

Now those are some screwed-up hires. While you may think that these are two colorful characters, there is someone in the company who is asking who hired these maniacs. Oops. That is where you come in. If you happen to be the sap who lived down to the hiring standards, then read on. Your weasel will show you the way on how to get yourself out of this screwed-up hiring mess.

Come Clean with it

With most normal hiring screw-ups, it is not too dangerous to come clean with it. You gave Ralph a chance. You thought he could do it. You checked out his resume and called his references. But, things didn't pan out. For most bad hires, this is a pretty acceptable logic trail. Your boss will agree and you move on with your life sans Ralph. It is very tidy and neat.

However, in the case where you have a freaking lunatic on your hands that is mowing down co-workers like some Dirty Harry movie, You can't say to your boss, "When Ralph put on his resume that he liked to do satanic rituals, I didn't think he was serious about it." Or not checking that Ralphie boy was the leader of a Nazi youth movement, may not sit too well with the powers that be.

In this case, you have unleashed the beast and this is more than the "give him a probationary period and then can him" situation. We are at Def Con 5 here. With every passing minute, this guy is wreaking havoc on the organization and people are looking for the idiot that put him in place. This is no time to come clean with it. You must move on and look for help.

Ignore It

Can you really ignore the first 30 minutes of *Saving Private Ryan*? This is the part where the troops storm Normandy Beach during WWII. It is one tough and graphic way to start a movie. Consider yourself on that beach right now, but instead of looking for Germans, you are looking for a madman masquerading as an employee.

By now, not only does everyone know about what is going on but your co-workers are either running for cover or rounding up a posse to get you and him. This one can't be dealt with by saying, "Oh, its just Ralph being an individual. Don't pay any attention to him."

Don't pay any attention to him!! Are you nuts? This is a guy who is feeding interns into the copier machine. He may be using the stapler gun as an Uzi. Or he has just melted down your servers leaving your company back in the telegraph era. Can you say "good night in black and white?"

There is just no way to ignore this maniac. He is a wild beast on the loose and must be dealt with. And we will deal with him. Please read on.

Blame it on Someone

Take it from the weasel. If you have a human resources department or even a part-time human resource person, you are in luck. The fickle finger of fate has found you a scapegoat. Use it and put the blame where it should be, right at the doorstep of the human resource group.

Everyone thinks that HR is worthless.

Most employees believe that human resource departments are worthless. Any department that has to dress itself up in fancy names is usually worthless. We deal in human capital. We are the cornerstone of the company. Yeah, and the garbage man is a waste services specialist. No matter what you call him, it still stinks. And so does the human resource department. These are the guys in school who are about three years in with no major and either end up in Human Resources or just give it up.

The Human Resource department should have caught this guy in their cosmic filter system, but they didn't. Perhaps they forgot to give this guy a psychological test or check his handwriting or his parole officer. If they had, this madman wouldn't be roaming the halls now, would he?

So, blaming it on the human resource department is your "Idiots Guide to How to Deal with a Screwed-up Hire." Perhaps, you like the people in human resources. Remember they did let you in. So, while they are an easy target, they are also wily about keeping their own jobs. They know the tricks and have those slimy workplace lawyers in their hip pocket. While human resource folks can be easy foil, they are tougher to kill than a flying cockroach.

All references lie.

Another easy target is to blame the references. This is even easier than the human resource group. Typically, a reference is from a company that competes with yours. So, they are always looking to stick you with their dirty laundry. Most of them can't wait to dump their trash on your doorstep. As the weasel says, "References are always liars." They really have no incentive to tell the truth and much more incentive to lie their heads off. If this maniac actually worked for them, do you feel they are proud of it?

"Yes, we were sorry to see Ralph go. He was such a free spirit but we had to downsize," says the reference liar. What he meant to say was, "Thank god we were able to cut loose this madman before he destroyed our IT department. He was playing a flute to see if he could make the wires on the server dance."

So, put the blame on someone else and keep your head down. That madman isn't out of your hair yet.

Make an Excuse

While placing blame is sure a convenient method to deal with your "maniac hire," so is making an excuse. Excuses are as plentiful as Starbucks and not nearly as expensive.

Our first excuse is the tried and true, "Who has the time to check references on people these days plus we know that all references lie anyway, so why check them." What we have here is the hiring conundrum. If you had the time, it wouldn't matter anyway. But, since your company needs a body now, here you go.

No one has time to check references.

What company has the luxury of time to sift through references, see 10 candidates, have them take personality and professional tests and go through the gauntlet of interviews? Why the company will be bankrupt by the time you go through all that. So, an easy excuse is as follows:
"Ted, why did you hire the madman in IT?"

"Hey, I had to plug a hole quickly. You know that the Munger project has a deadline of this Friday, so we took the first available body."

"You do know that there are orangutans that seem to be smarter than this guy?"

"If you are so concerned, then you see who you come up with in a day."

And with that, you turn and walk quickly away. The "not enough time" excuse is a timeless one. Get it!! OK, that was pretty lame but you get the idea. There is never enough time to make a great hiring decision. You just do the best you can do.

The time excuse can be a handy one in many ways. You may not have had enough time to meet with the candidate. So, you can quickly focus the blame on the process with a simple:

"Yes, I was out of town when the 'maniac' made the rounds. All he saw was Gamble."

Here you can get a two for one or a two-fer. You are a busy guy so you can't possibly see every loser who troops through your godforsaken company. Secondly, you can add a total loser to the sentence and blame it on his judgment. Now you are perceived as too busy to be in this loop and you can push it to another loser, like Gamble. This is the hiring equivalent of "birds of a feather, flock together." In this case, it is "losers are likely to hire other losers."

Another great excuse is to blame it on the quota system. Most companies have hiring quotas. Most companies want a diverse employee base, but they usually go about it in such a lame way that they end up with weird quotas. For example, is it really your fault there are no Eskimos in accounting? I wouldn't take my gloves off if I lived in Alaska, either. But, someone has said that in the name of diversity, we need an Eskimo in accounting. You try finding an Eskimo who can knock out a spreadsheet in a week.

Every company has some sort of quota to fill.

So, the other great excuse is to blame it on the quota system.

"Ted, you know that you hired a maniac in accounting."

"Yes sir, but he does fill our diversity requirements. There are just not too many serial killers in accounting to pick from."

And there you have it. Game. Set. Match. No one argues, or even gets close to getting involved in a company's quest for diversity. Use that to your advantage when you can. It is the safest move you have.

These are some of the top excuses in the game. I am sure that there are many others. But, try not to get too exotic with your excuses on making a hiring mistake. If you do, you will find that someone will feel that you are a mistake too.

Deny It

It may be tough to deny that there is a madman roaming the halls of your organization. When corporations had offices and lots of floors, it might have been an easier way out. But, in the age of cubicles and computers, everyone knows everything. So, the traditional method of denial may not be your salvation.

However, you may want to do some misdirecting. This will work until you get the gumption to either blame it on someone else or to find a good excuse. Fortunately, you are in luck. We have just the diversion for you.

Everyone transfers a problem to another department.

The simplest diversion is the "not my department" gambit. Even though you may have hired the madman, you conveniently transfer him to another department. Now, he is someone else's problem. And you are off the hook. In fact, you can even use the bravado of "I knew that this guy was a loser but IT thought he would be a good fit for them." The old bait and switch works in hiring mistakes just as it works in selling cars.

You may not have a big enough company to do the transfer gambit. In that case, you have no one to transfer this problem to. However, you still have a way of denying that he works for you. You pose him as another company training exercise. In fact, in this case, you can actually reward someone for bringing this guy to your attention.

"Ted, there is a madman roaming the halls. Why, in god's name did you hire this guy?"

And you respond thusly, "I am so glad you brought this to my attention so quickly. We hired this guy to demonstrate what not to look for in an employee. And you spotted it right off the bat. Great job."

There you have it. Every company does inane training. Mock drills and simulations are nothing new and they are actually encouraged in some demented organizations. Use this to your advantage and make every sorry hire another training exercise. Pretty soon, people will be waiting for you to spring another one on them. Then it won't matter who you hire. Your track record of spotless training exercises speaks for itself.

Simply Quit

Are you kidding? Don't even let the thought cross your mind. Not when you have plenty of people to blame, excuses to be used and even ways of turning a bad hire into an ongoing training exercise.

My god, you have so much fodder here, even you can stay employed and likely get a raise if you listen to the weasel. Quit, indeed. I think not. Even though it is tempting to quit an organization that would hire the likes of you, don't kill the golden goose.

If this company not only hired you, but let's you hire others, you couldn't ask for a better place to work. This is cupcake incorporated and you should thank your lucky stars to be in such a worthless place. But, hey, it is your worthless place and you have your job and dignity. What more do you want?

Chapter 10

You've Signed Something You Shouldn't Have

Wasn't it neat when you first learned to write your name in cursive script? Do you remember that day? You felt like such a big person. Why, you could write your name like adults did. It made you proud. Little did you know that learning to write your name distinctively would bite you in the rear twenty years later?

But there you are. You've signed some sort of document that is now careening around your office screaming "screw-up." What was once such an innocent thing as signing one's name has now become a fight for corporate survival.

You are not the only person to sign something that you later regretted. Can you imagine how the guy felt after he signed the Louisiana Purchase? He gave about 25% of the United States away for $1.00 Now, some will say that he actually got the better of the deal. Have you ever been to Louisiana? But, regardless of your preference for or against swamps, decadence and fine dining, you have to admit that Louisiana and its surrounding area is worth just a tad more than a buck.

We are talking about signing something that is so stupid and that will add so much pain to the organization, it is laughable. It is one of those documents, typically some contract, where you really wonder who in their right mind would sign something like that.

Here is a great example. Some bonehead in Detroit signed a contract that authorized the payment of assembly line workers even though they weren't working. In an attempt to get the unions off their backs, those auto moguls decided that it was as good to pay these guys no matter what they did or didn't do. And you wonder why the Japanese dominate the domestic auto market? Look no further than this contract signed by some dunderhead in Detroit.

Did you ever wonder why there are so many peanuts on airplane flights? Why can't there be cashews or gum or cookies? My guess is that some airline dolt signed a contract with the peanut guy that gave them the rights to have peanuts on their flights until the year 3000. They locked in some long-term peanut deal to keep those nuts inexpensive, while we are clamoring for a bit more nourishment.

I always wondered if in the boardrooms of the big airlines someone might bring up the fact that their customers are craving more than peanuts.

"You know, it might be nice to offer something other than peanuts to our frequent customers. If you fly once a week, you will have eaten over 100 bags of peanuts in a year."

"Tell that to Anderson. He is the one who signed that peanut deal until the year 3000. We even called every zoo in the country and they won't take them either."

Unfortunately, when you were little, signing your name was just signing your name. Now, signing your name means that you are actually authorizing something to be done. In your case, let's face it, you shouldn't be allowed to sign anything unless it is in crayon. But, you have signed something and now people are looking at you like they look at Anderson.

"There goes 'Peanut' Anderson. That's the guy you can thank for all those damn peanut flights. Way to go, nut boy."

The problem with the signature is that it is something others can hold in the air like a prize possession. It screams loser and it may scream the death of your career. But, fear not, your John Hancock won't go down in a blaze of infamy. Your trusty weasel will come to the rescue.

Let's get to the bottom of this mess and straighten it out. You should know the drill by now. We will go through the options quicker than the drying ink on a flaming contract.

Come Clean With it

"Well, boss, I just signed a contract giving the vendor the right to over half our profits. I just wanted to let you know before the bill hits your desk."

Excuse me. Just how is that statement going to help you? I know that it has this twinge of integrity to it. However, your integrity is totally trumped by your idiocy. This isn't some dinky agreement that you have somehow managed to sign. This is your version of the Magna Carta. Only, this time it might as well be the Magna Dumba.

The only way to come clean in this case is to admit to some severe medical condition. Perhaps dyslexia would be a good one to try to surface. I thought that those series of millions were really ones. In my stated condition, it was truly what I thought.

Let's face it. Coming clean with it in this case is pretty weak stuff. You are not throwing a 90-mile-an-hour fastball here. In effect, if you come clean with it, you are admitting that either you can't or won't read. Worse yet, is that if you can read, you can't comprehend anything. Worse still, is that if you can read and comprehend the document, that you somehow had the most incredible sense of poor judgment to sign the bloody thing.

No, my friend, coming clean with this one is truly the kiss of death. I don't care if you do bring in a note from your doctor or your mother that states that you have some sort of medical condition that renders your judgment in these matters moot. That form ain't going to fly here. You will be laughed off the planet and certainly out of the office. Can you imagine the stories that your former co-workers would tell about you.

"Anderson pulled an incredible blunder by signing the peanut agreement. Can you believe that he actually had some bogus medical form saying that he couldn't comprehend anything more than two sentences at a time? This guy is a moron and a total putz."

You don't want to pull an Anderson, do you? Then please read on. There is a way out of this mess without resorting to cutting off your hands.

Ignore It

Anderson tried to ignore his peanut mistake. I made up the doctors note to make a point. But, you still see those damn peanuts on every flight, don't you? These are things that are difficult to ignore. Once you sign something of this magnitude, it takes on a life of its own.

The only way to walk ever so quietly away from this one is if you know that there is significant lag time between when a contract is signed and when it will be executed. This does give you and a certain weasel time to plot some strategy. So, don't panic. No one begins anything the minute that it is signed. And that piece of wisdom gives you tons of opportunity to change the course of your misguided actions.

There's always a lag time between contract and execution.

If you know immediately that you have made the world's biggest blunder, call up the vendor whose contract you have signed and demand that he send it back. Or quickly type up another document that counteracts the contract and send it immediately to him. Try the paper chase gambit. Pepper this poor bastard with paperwork. Turn his office into a blizzard and when you have total white out, sneak out into the darkness. Remember, never go into the light.

Ignoring, in this case, means actively ignoring and weaseling at the same time. A total ignore will suddenly turn ugly when an elephant shows up in your boss's office unannounced.

"What the *@#$ is this elephant doing in my office," your boss says sweetly.

"Why Anderson signed a contract to have that delivered," says your not so sweet administrative assistant.

And you don't have to have a big imagination to see where this story is going. Let's just say that you won't be in this story much longer at the company. Oh, but you will be the story for years to come. Now, that is not what you want. Is it? Please read on.

Blame it on someone else

Now you are talking. The blame game in this case is so easy, it is almost like you used invisible ink to sign your life away. Look no further than your favorite weasel for this one. The world is filled with lawyers. Lawyers are the true definition of a weasel. Blame it on them.

Everyone hates lawyers. They are true slime and everyone knows it.

No one will ever take a lawyer's side in anything. They are the most hated profession in the world. They speak in tongues that only other lawyers understand. That is how they charge those ungodly fees. If they would put things in common sense terms, who would need them? But they write contracts in a language that seems like it is from another planet. Who can really understand that stuff? I'll tell you who. Another weasel lawyer can, that's who.

Now, you have your choice of how to place blame at the foot of the legal community. Here are some sample dialogues you can have that not only will protect you from harm but will have your co-workers nodding in total agreement.

"That damn lawyer put in a fine print clause I couldn't read."

"Our legal counsel should have caught that fine print."

Any type of blame can be put at the foot of the legal community and it will be heartfelt and taken well. Everyone has some form of hatred for a lawyer. Just look at our divorce rate.

No one understands a contract except for lawyers.

The only downside of blaming the incident on lawyers is that those same lawyers can sue your rear end. Unfortunately, they typically have little qualm about doing just that. It is their make-up to sue and sue they must. So, while the lawyers are a great alibi; remember that all judges were once lawyers. It just doesn't seem fair, now, does it?

You can blame it on others who should have advised you or other team members who are now mocking you. But, there are other ways out of this contract conundrum.

Make an Excuse

There are a million valid reasons why you signed something you shouldn't have. And many of them actually might get you off the hook. First off, you don't have the background or ability to sign a document that gives anyone any authority. Is your company insane? How can they give someone like you any say so in company policy?

Check what is a real legal document.

This brings me to one piece of sage weasel wisdom. If you are not an officer of the company then you may not be legally be bound to this contract. Yep, your signature may mean nothing unless you are an officer of the firm. You can skate. If your company has half a brain, you are not likely an officer of the company. Pray that you work for a company that recognizes mediocrity when it sees it.

But our company is passing out titles like you pass out Tums at a Chinese restaurant. You may work for a bank or an advertising agency where everyone is a Vice-President or has some sort of lordly title. It turns out that just because you have some pompous title, your signature doesn't mean squat. This is particularly true if you are with a private company. Only those who own part of the company can be on the hook for a contract. So, if you are a Vice-President of a private company, but not an owner, your title may not be worth the paper it is printed on. Thank goodness. You have all the big headed perks and none of the responsibility. Life is good. Unfortunately, to ensure that this wisdom is really true, you will have to consult with a lawyer. Ironic, isn't it.

So, let's say that you are the poor bastard that doesn't fit the profile above. Boy, did your company ever make a mistake with you. However, because you are clearly incompetent, you can use that to your advantage. I am sure that you didn't have the time or training to deal with such a complex document. What better excuse is there than to blame the company itself. If they hired you, you know that they can't be too good. So, lay it on them. You deserve training. You didn't get it. How can you be expected to understand that legal mumbo jumbo without any training?

Frankly, who has time to go over that stuff anyway? We have things to do. Time is wasting. If you ponder every peccadillo of this contract, it may be too late. You have things to do and this is just getting in the way.

So, pick your excuse. There must be one of these that fits the bill. If not, there is always denial.

Deny It

Have you ever seen those television shows where some shady secretary sneaks in a document or page that needs a signature and hides it among other normal papers? The busy boss signs up a storm and then all hell breaks loose. Naturally, the boss denies that he knowingly signed this dastardly document and the ensuing finger pointing drama fills up another half hour of mindless television.

Denying that you have actually signed a contract is a classic defense that it boggles the mind. You don't have to claim that you were duped into signing it like the example above. You simply just deny that you signed it. I mean, if no one actually saw you sign the document, then how do they really know it was you?

Who can really prove it was you, anyway? No, this isn't a test. The answer is no one. It is a clean, safe story. To cap it off, you might even say that you wouldn't be allowed to sign such a document of this magnitude. If you are as incompetent as I think you are, everyone will agree with this. Case closed. Here is some of the hallway talk that might transpire:

"They say that the contract giving Hamas control of our IT group was signed by Briscoe. Come on, there is no way that the boss let's Briscoe sign something like that. Something just isn't right."

So, the denial based on no one seeing you actually sign this turkey is a very sweet alibi. It should set off a series of inquisitions about who might have mistakenly given you this document to sign. It will make the Spanish Inquisition look like a tea party. This only works if you signed this in the confines of your own cubicle. But, suppose that in a fit of looking important, you asked all your colleagues to witness this signing.

"Can you believe that they allowed me to sign this contract? The boss really thinks that I must be senior management material," you say with pride.

And with that you sign the contract with a flourish and now a terrorist leader is calling your boss to negotiate control of the company's IT department. That is not the ending you were looking for, now is it? So, if you get carried away with the ceremonial signing, you can always fall back on another denial gambit. That is the wrong contract or other contract denial.

"I did sign a contract with Havas, but not Hamas."

The key to this defense is to admit that you actually signed a contract but deny that you signed this particular contract. Most companies have so many contracts going through the pipeline that it is easy to see that there might have been a mix up. And that is what you are counting on for this denial. Let's face it; it had to be a mix up since you were actually signing a contract that had some meaning to it.

If all else fails, deny it with the loss of memory. I would imagine that this would fit you to a tee. Hey, you forget things all the time. It is a wonder that you can remember where you cubicle is.

"I just don't remember signing that contract. I mean, I usually don't sign contracts and I just can't imagine when I signed this one."

How can someone argue with this? That is unless you staged some ceremonial party in honor of signing something. Otherwise, you are right as rain. Since you shouldn't be signing them in the first place, the boss will either assume that it was someone else trying to frame you or that you were in your typical "slug-like" state and really didn't recall what you were doing. Either way, you are likely to be off the hook. Who says that it there isn't an upside to being considered incompetent?

Quit

Don't even think about quitting if you signed something that you shouldn't have. There are so many ways out of this paper chase that only signing something in blood should be a consideration for quitting. Even then, you should have someone do a DNA check. If it goes to a bogus lab, you can even beat this wrap.

The only way that you should ever consider quitting is if you feel that you can use it to get a better job at the competition. Knowledge can be power. Knowing that there is a signed contract that might take your company down can be a good knowledge chip for getting in with the competition. Every competitor wants to know what the other one is doing. Who knows, they might think that dealing with a terrorist cell is an excellent international move. Your blunder might be considered a vanguard move by the competition.

"This Briscoe is brilliant. Can you believe that he engineered a contract with Hamas? Even the President of the U.S. can't do that. This is a must hire guy."

So, quit my eye. Signing a bad piece of parchment might just be the best career move you have ever made. Regardless, if you stay or go, you will live to see another day. That is exactly what our weasel promises. Keep your job and your dignity. For most of you, one out of two ain't bad.

978-0-595-45370-2
0-595-45370-8

Made in the USA